The golden egg

Story written by Alison Hawes
Illustrated by Tim Archbold

Speed Sounds

Consonants

Ask your child to say the sounds (not the letter names) clearly and quickly, in and out of order. Make sure he or she does not add 'uh' to the end of the sounds, e.g. 'f' not 'fuh'.

Each box contains one sound. Focus sounds for this story are circled.

f	l	m	n	r	s	v	z	sh	th	ng
ff	**ll**	mm	nn	rr	ss	ve	zz			nk
ph	le	mb	kn	wr	**se**		se			
			gn		c		s			
					ce					

b	c	d	g	h	j	p	qu	t	w	x	y	ch
bb	k	dd	gg		g	**pp**		tt	wh			tch
	ck		gu		**ge**							
					dge							

Vowels

Ask your child to say the sounds in and out of order.

a	e ea	i	o	u	ay	ee y	igh i	ow o
at	h**e**n	**i**n	**o**n	**u**p	d**ay**	s**ee**	h**igh**	bl**ow**

oo	oo	ar	**or** **oor** **ore**	air	ir	ou	oy oi
z**oo**	l**oo**k	c**ar**	f**or**	f**air**	wh**ir**l	sh**ou**t	b**oy**

Story Green Words

For each word ask your child to read the separate sounds, e.g. 'b-u-s', 'p-oo-l' and then blend sounds together to make the word, e.g. 'bus', 'pool'. Sometimes one sound is represented by more than one letter, e.g. 'th', 'oo'. These are underlined.

corn poor goose barn large fled laid make

Ask your child to say the syllables and then read the whole word.

morn|ing orch|ard mar|ket to|morr|ow gold|en*

Ask your child to read the root first and then the whole word with the suffix.

pass → passed sudden → suddenly own → owned

horse → horses order → ordered peer → peered*

* *Challenge Words*

Vocabulary Check

Tell your child the meaning of each word in the context of the story.

	definition:	sentence:
orchard	*a group of fruit trees*	*... the man passed through the orchard on his way to the barn.*
gloomy	*fed up*	*The man felt gloomy...*
glinted	*shiny flashes of light*	*A bright light glinted in the darkness...*
peered	*looked closely*	*He peered into the goose's nest...*
fled	*ran away scared*	*She... fled far, far away!*

Red Words

Red words don't sound like they look. Ask your child to read the words but if he or she gets stuck read the word to your child.

said	by	saw	would
put	how	all	old
through	who	where	small
once	does	there	me
what	would	no	one

The golden egg

Do not read the story to your child first. Point to the words as your child reads. If your child gets stuck on a word help him or her say the sounds and blend them together. Re-read each sentence to your child to help him or her remember what he or she has read. Discuss what is happening on each page.

There was once a man who owned a small farm. He was so poor he had very little food to feed his animals.

One by one, he sold his horses, sheep and geese.

Before long, all he had left was a single goose and a small bag of corn.

One morning, the man passed through the orchard on his way to the barn. He was going to feed his last goose.

The man felt gloomy as he fed the goose the last of the corn. “Soon you must be sold, too,” he said.

Suddenly, the man stopped. A bright light glinted in the darkness of the barn. What *was* it?

He peered into the goose's nest, and there he saw a large golden egg. He sat on the hay, in shock.

"This golden egg will make me very rich!" the man said to himself.

The next morning the man ran to the barn. He peered into the goose's nest.

"Hurray!" he said, happily. "A second golden egg! I will sell my eggs to make me rich. Soon I shall have a farm with lots of horses, sheep and geese!"

The man ran all the way to the market to sell his golden eggs.

The next morning the man ran to the barn.
He peered into the goose's nest.
As before, there was one golden egg in the nest.
But the man wanted more.

"You are too *slow* at laying eggs," the man grumbled to the goose.
"Tomorrow, lay me lots more golden eggs!" he ordered.

But the next day, as before, there was just one egg in the nest.

"How will I get back my horses, sheep and geese if you lay me just one egg a day?" the man said.

"You must lay *more* eggs, you must!" he yelled angrily.

The goose was frightened by the man's yelling. She was so frightened that she ran into the orchard, flapped her wings and fled far, far away!

The man looked high and low for the goose, but she was nowhere to be seen.

The man put his head in his hands.
He would have no horses, sheep or geese... and he had lost the goose that laid the golden eggs.

Now ask your child to re-read the story helping him or her think about the best way to read each sentence.

Questions to talk about

Read the questions aloud to your child and ask him or her to find the answers on the relevant pages. Do not ask your child to read the questions – the words are harder than he or she can read at the moment.

p.9 What did the man sell?

p.10 Why did the man feel gloomy?

p.11 What was glinting in the darkness?

p.11 The man thought the egg would make him rich. Why did he think this?

p.12 The man ran all the way to the market. Why do you think he did this?

p.14 Why was the man angry with the goose?

p.15 How do you think the man felt at the end?

Questions to read and answer

Ask your child to read the questions and find the correct answer in the story.

1. The man's farm was **big / small / large**.

2. The goose was in **the barn / the tree / the street**.

3. The golden eggs would make the man **poor / old / rich**.

4. The man sold the eggs at **a shop / the market / his farm**.

5. At the end the man had **lots of golden eggs / lots of animals / lost his goose**.

Speedy Green Words

Ask your child to read the words clearly and quickly – across the rows, down the columns, and in and out of order.

before	eggs	too	dark
food	sheep	stopped	more
day	soon	little	high
slow	left	last	farm
this	very	light	feed